Monday	

Tuesday	

Wednesday	

Thursday	

Friday	

Saturday	

Sunday	

Places to Go

☐
☐
☐
☐
☐
☐

People to See

☐
☐
☐
☐
☐
☐

Things to Do

☐
☐
☐
☐
☐
☐
☐
☐
☐
☐
☐
☐
☐

Special Reminders

☐
☐
☐
☐
☐
☐
☐

Monday	

Tuesday	

Wednesday	

Thursday	

Friday	

Saturday	

Sunday	

Places to Go

People to See

Things to Do

Special Reminders

| **Monday** | |

| **Tuesday** | |

| **Wednesday** | |

| **Thursday** | |

| **Friday** | |

| **Saturday** | |

| **Sunday** | |

Places to Go

☐ ___________________
☐ ___________________
☐ ___________________
☐ ___________________
☐ ___________________
☐ ___________________

People to See

☐ ___________________
☐ ___________________
☐ ___________________
☐ ___________________
☐ ___________________
☐ ___________________

Things to Do

☐ ___________________
☐ ___________________
☐ ___________________
☐ ___________________
☐ ___________________
☐ ___________________
☐ ___________________
☐ ___________________
☐ ___________________
☐ ___________________
☐ ___________________
☐ ___________________
☐ ___________________

Special Reminders

☐ ___________________
☐ ___________________
☐ ___________________
☐ ___________________
☐ ___________________
☐ ___________________
☐ ___________________

Monday	

Tuesday	

Wednesday	

Thursday	

Friday	

Saturday	

Sunday	

Places to Go

☐
☐
☐
☐
☐
☐

People to See

☐
☐
☐
☐
☐
☐

Things to Do

☐
☐
☐
☐
☐
☐
☐
☐
☐
☐
☐
☐
☐
☐

Special Reminders

☐
☐
☐
☐
☐
☐
☐

Monday	

Places to Go

- ☐
- ☐
- ☐
- ☐
- ☐
- ☐

Tuesday	

People to See

- ☐
- ☐
- ☐
- ☐
- ☐
- ☐

Wednesday	

Things to Do

- ☐
- ☐
- ☐
- ☐
- ☐

Thursday	

- ☐
- ☐
- ☐
- ☐
- ☐
- ☐
- ☐
- ☐

Friday	

Saturday	

Special Reminders

- ☐
- ☐
- ☐
- ☐
- ☐
- ☐
- ☐

Sunday	

Monday

Tuesday

Wednesday

Thursday

Friday

Saturday

Sunday

Places to Go

☐
☐
☐
☐
☐
☐
☐

People to See

☐
☐
☐
☐
☐
☐

Things to Do

☐
☐
☐
☐
☐
☐
☐
☐
☐
☐
☐
☐
☐
☐

Special Reminders

☐
☐
☐
☐
☐
☐
☐

Monday	

Tuesday	

Wednesday	

Thursday	

Friday	

Saturday	

Sunday	

Places to Go

People to See

Things to Do

Special Reminders

Monday	

Tuesday	

Wednesday	

Thursday	

Friday	

Saturday	

Sunday	

Places to Go

- ☐
- ☐
- ☐
- ☐
- ☐
- ☐

People to See

- ☐
- ☐
- ☐
- ☐
- ☐
- ☐

Things to Do

- ☐
- ☐
- ☐
- ☐
- ☐
- ☐
- ☐
- ☐
- ☐
- ☐
- ☐
- ☐
- ☐
- ☐

Special Reminders

- ☐
- ☐
- ☐
- ☐
- ☐
- ☐
- ☐

Monday	

Tuesday	

Wednesday	

Thursday	

Friday	

Saturday	

Sunday	

Places to Go

☐ ___________________________
☐ ___________________________
☐ ___________________________
☐ ___________________________
☐ ___________________________
☐ ___________________________

People to See

☐ ___________________________
☐ ___________________________
☐ ___________________________
☐ ___________________________
☐ ___________________________
☐ ___________________________

Things to Do

☐ ___________________________
☐ ___________________________
☐ ___________________________
☐ ___________________________
☐ ___________________________
☐ ___________________________
☐ ___________________________
☐ ___________________________
☐ ___________________________
☐ ___________________________
☐ ___________________________

Special Reminders

☐ ___________________________
☐ ___________________________
☐ ___________________________
☐ ___________________________
☐ ___________________________
☐ ___________________________
☐ ___________________________

| **Monday** | |
| | |

| **Tuesday** | |
| | |

| **Wednesday** | |
| | |

| **Thursday** | |
| | |

| **Friday** | |
| | |

| **Saturday** | |
| | |

| **Sunday** | |
| | |

Places to Go

- ☐
- ☐
- ☐
- ☐
- ☐
- ☐
- ☐

People to See

- ☐
- ☐
- ☐
- ☐
- ☐
- ☐

Things to Do

- ☐
- ☐
- ☐
- ☐
- ☐
- ☐
- ☐
- ☐
- ☐
- ☐
- ☐
- ☐
- ☐
- ☐

Special Reminders

- ☐
- ☐
- ☐
- ☐
- ☐
- ☐

Monday	

Tuesday	

Wednesday	

Thursday	

Friday	

Saturday	

Sunday	

Places to Go

- ☐
- ☐
- ☐
- ☐
- ☐
- ☐

People to See

- ☐
- ☐
- ☐
- ☐
- ☐
- ☐

Things to Do

- ☐
- ☐
- ☐
- ☐
- ☐
- ☐
- ☐
- ☐
- ☐
- ☐
- ☐
- ☐
- ☐

Special Reminders

- ☐
- ☐
- ☐
- ☐
- ☐
- ☐
- ☐

Monday

Tuesday

Wednesday

Thursday

Friday

Saturday

Sunday

Places to Go

People to See

Things to Do

Special Reminders

Monday	

Tuesday	

Wednesday	

Thursday	

Friday	

Saturday	

Sunday	

Places to Go

☐ ___________________
☐ ___________________
☐ ___________________
☐ ___________________
☐ ___________________
☐ ___________________

People to See

☐ ___________________
☐ ___________________
☐ ___________________
☐ ___________________
☐ ___________________
☐ ___________________

Things to Do

☐ ___________________
☐ ___________________
☐ ___________________
☐ ___________________
☐ ___________________
☐ ___________________
☐ ___________________
☐ ___________________
☐ ___________________
☐ ___________________
☐ ___________________
☐ ___________________

Special Reminders

☐ ___________________
☐ ___________________
☐ ___________________
☐ ___________________
☐ ___________________
☐ ___________________

| **Monday** | |

| **Tuesday** | |

| **Wednesday** | |

| **Thursday** | |

| **Friday** | |

| **Saturday** | |

| **Sunday** | |

Places to Go

People to See

Things to Do

Special Reminders

<table>
<tr><td>

Monday

Tuesday

Wednesday

Thursday

Friday

Saturday

Sunday

</td><td>

Places to Go

☐ _______________
☐ _______________
☐ _______________
☐ _______________
☐ _______________
☐ _______________

People to See

☐ _______________
☐ _______________
☐ _______________
☐ _______________
☐ _______________
☐ _______________

Things to Do

☐ _______________
☐ _______________
☐ _______________
☐ _______________
☐ _______________
☐ _______________
☐ _______________
☐ _______________
☐ _______________
☐ _______________
☐ _______________
☐ _______________

Special Reminders

☐ _______________
☐ _______________
☐ _______________
☐ _______________
☐ _______________
☐ _______________

</td></tr>
</table>

Monday

Tuesday

Wednesday

Thursday

Friday

Saturday

Sunday

Places to Go

People to See

Things to Do

Special Reminders

Monday

Tuesday

Wednesday

Thursday

Friday

Saturday

Sunday

Places to Go

People to See

Things to Do

Special Reminders

| **Monday** | |

| **Tuesday** | |

| **Wednesday** | |

| **Thursday** | |

| **Friday** | |

| **Saturday** | |

| **Sunday** | |

Places to Go

People to See

Things to Do

Special Reminders

Monday

Tuesday

Wednesday

Thursday

Friday

Saturday

Sunday

Places to Go

People to See

Things to Do

Special Reminders

Monday

Tuesday

Wednesday

Thursday

Friday

Saturday

Sunday

Places to Go

People to See

Things to Do

Special Reminders

Monday	

Tuesday	

Wednesday	

Thursday	

Friday	

Saturday	

Sunday	

Places to Go

- ☐
- ☐
- ☐
- ☐
- ☐
- ☐

People to See

- ☐
- ☐
- ☐
- ☐
- ☐
- ☐

Things to Do

- ☐
- ☐
- ☐
- ☐
- ☐
- ☐
- ☐
- ☐
- ☐
- ☐
- ☐
- ☐
- ☐

Special Reminders

- ☐
- ☐
- ☐
- ☐
- ☐
- ☐
- ☐

| **Monday** | |

| **Tuesday** | |

| **Wednesday** | |

| **Thursday** | |

| **Friday** | |

| **Saturday** | |

| **Sunday** | |

Places to Go

People to See

Things to Do

Special Reminders

Monday	

Tuesday	

Wednesday	

Thursday	

Friday	

Saturday	

Sunday	

Places to Go

People to See

Things to Do

Special Reminders

Monday	

Tuesday	

Wednesday	

Thursday	

Friday	

Saturday	

Sunday	

Places to Go

People to See

Things to Do

Special Reminders

| **Monday** | |

| **Tuesday** | |

| **Wednesday** | |

| **Thursday** | |

| **Friday** | |

| **Saturday** | |

| **Sunday** | |

Places to Go

☐
☐
☐
☐
☐
☐

People to See

☐
☐
☐
☐
☐
☐

Things to Do

☐
☐
☐
☐
☐
☐
☐
☐
☐
☐
☐
☐
☐

Special Reminders

☐
☐
☐
☐
☐
☐
☐

Monday

Tuesday

Wednesday

Thursday

Friday

Saturday

Sunday

Places to Go

People to See

Things to Do

Special Reminders

Monday

Tuesday

Wednesday

Thursday

Friday

Saturday

Sunday

Places to Go

People to See

Things to Do

Special Reminders

Monday

Tuesday

Wednesday

Thursday

Friday

Saturday

Sunday

Places to Go

People to See

Things to Do

Special Reminders

| **Monday** | |

| **Tuesday** | |

| **Wednesday** | |

| **Thursday** | |

| **Friday** | |

| **Saturday** | |

| **Sunday** | |

Places to Go

People to See

Things to Do

Special Reminders

| **Monday** | |

| **Tuesday** | |

| **Wednesday** | |

| **Thursday** | |

| **Friday** | |

| **Saturday** | |

| **Sunday** | |

Places to Go

☐
☐
☐
☐
☐
☐
☐

People to See

☐
☐
☐
☐
☐
☐

Things to Do

☐
☐
☐
☐
☐
☐
☐
☐
☐
☐
☐
☐
☐
☐
☐

Special Reminders

☐
☐
☐
☐
☐
☐
☐

<table>
<tr><td>

Monday

Tuesday

Wednesday

Thursday

Friday

Saturday

Sunday

</td><td>

Places to Go

☐ ______________________
☐ ______________________
☐ ______________________
☐ ______________________
☐ ______________________
☐ ______________________

People to See

☐ ______________________
☐ ______________________
☐ ______________________
☐ ______________________
☐ ______________________
☐ ______________________

Things to Do

☐ ______________________
☐ ______________________
☐ ______________________
☐ ______________________
☐ ______________________
☐ ______________________
☐ ______________________
☐ ______________________
☐ ______________________
☐ ______________________
☐ ______________________
☐ ______________________
☐ ______________________

Special Reminders

☐ ______________________
☐ ______________________
☐ ______________________
☐ ______________________
☐ ______________________
☐ ______________________
☐ ______________________

</td></tr>
</table>

Monday

Tuesday

Wednesday

Thursday

Friday

Saturday

Sunday

Places to Go

People to See

Things to Do

Special Reminders

Monday

Tuesday

Wednesday

Thursday

Friday

Saturday

Sunday

Places to Go

People to See

Things to Do

Special Reminders

<table>
<tr><td>

Monday

Tuesday

Wednesday

Thursday

Friday

Saturday

Sunday

</td><td>

Places to Go

☐
☐
☐
☐
☐
☐
☐

People to See

☐
☐
☐
☐
☐
☐

Things to Do

☐
☐
☐
☐
☐
☐
☐
☐
☐
☐
☐
☐
☐
☐

Special Reminders

☐
☐
☐
☐
☐
☐
☐

</td></tr>
</table>

Monday	

Tuesday	

Wednesday	

Thursday	

Friday	

Saturday	

Sunday	

Places to Go

☐
☐
☐
☐
☐
☐

People to See

☐
☐
☐
☐
☐
☐

Things to Do

☐
☐
☐
☐
☐
☐
☐
☐
☐
☐
☐
☐
☐
☐

Special Reminders

☐
☐
☐
☐
☐
☐

| **Monday** | |

| **Tuesday** | |

| **Wednesday** | |

| **Thursday** | |

| **Friday** | |

| **Saturday** | |

| **Sunday** | |

Places to Go

People to See

Things to Do

Special Reminders

Monday	

Tuesday	

Wednesday	

Thursday	

Friday	

Saturday	

Sunday	

Places to Go

- ☐
- ☐
- ☐
- ☐
- ☐
- ☐

People to See

- ☐
- ☐
- ☐
- ☐
- ☐
- ☐

Things to Do

- ☐
- ☐
- ☐
- ☐
- ☐
- ☐
- ☐
- ☐
- ☐
- ☐
- ☐
- ☐
- ☐

Special Reminders

- ☐
- ☐
- ☐
- ☐
- ☐
- ☐
- ☐

Monday	

Tuesday	

Wednesday	

Thursday	

Friday	

Saturday	

Sunday	

Places to Go

☐ ________________________
☐ ________________________
☐ ________________________
☐ ________________________
☐ ________________________
☐ ________________________
☐ ________________________

People to See

☐ ________________________
☐ ________________________
☐ ________________________
☐ ________________________
☐ ________________________
☐ ________________________

Things to Do

☐ ________________________
☐ ________________________
☐ ________________________
☐ ________________________
☐ ________________________
☐ ________________________
☐ ________________________
☐ ________________________
☐ ________________________
☐ ________________________
☐ ________________________
☐ ________________________
☐ ________________________
☐ ________________________

Special Reminders

☐ ________________________
☐ ________________________
☐ ________________________
☐ ________________________
☐ ________________________
☐ ________________________
☐ ________________________

Monday	

Tuesday	

Wednesday	

Thursday	

Friday	

Saturday	

Sunday	

Places to Go

People to See

Things to Do

Special Reminders

| **Monday** | |

| **Tuesday** | |

| **Wednesday** | |

| **Thursday** | |

| **Friday** | |

| **Saturday** | |

| **Sunday** | |

Places to Go

☐
☐
☐
☐
☐
☐
☐

People to See

☐
☐
☐
☐
☐
☐

Things to Do

☐
☐
☐
☐
☐
☐
☐
☐
☐
☐
☐
☐
☐

Special Reminders

☐
☐
☐
☐
☐
☐
☐

Monday

Tuesday

Wednesday

Thursday

Friday

Saturday

Sunday

Places to Go

People to See

Things to Do

Special Reminders

Monday	Places to Go
Tuesday	People to See
Wednesday	Things to Do
Thursday	
Friday	
Saturday	Special Reminders
Sunday	

Monday

Tuesday

Wednesday

Thursday

Friday

Saturday

Sunday

Places to Go

People to See

Things to Do

Special Reminders

Monday

Tuesday

Wednesday

Thursday

Friday

Saturday

Sunday

Places to Go

People to See

Things to Do

Special Reminders

Monday

Tuesday

Wednesday

Thursday

Friday

Saturday

Sunday

Places to Go

People to See

Things to Do

Special Reminders

Monday

Tuesday

Wednesday

Thursday

Friday

Saturday

Sunday

Places to Go

- [ ]
- [ ]
- [ ]
- [ ]
- [ ]
- [ ]

People to See

- [ ]
- [ ]
- [ ]
- [ ]
- [ ]
- [ ]

Things to Do

- [ ]
- [ ]
- [ ]
- [ ]
- [ ]
- [ ]
- [ ]
- [ ]
- [ ]
- [ ]
- [ ]
- [ ]
- [ ]

Special Reminders

- [ ]
- [ ]
- [ ]
- [ ]
- [ ]
- [ ]
- [ ]

Monday

Tuesday

Wednesday

Thursday

Friday

Saturday

Sunday

Places to Go

- ☐
- ☐
- ☐
- ☐
- ☐
- ☐

People to See

- ☐
- ☐
- ☐
- ☐
- ☐
- ☐

Things to Do

- ☐
- ☐
- ☐
- ☐
- ☐
- ☐
- ☐
- ☐
- ☐
- ☐
- ☐
- ☐
- ☐
- ☐

Special Reminders

- ☐
- ☐
- ☐
- ☐
- ☐
- ☐
- ☐

Monday		Places to Go

Tuesday		People to See

Wednesday		Things to Do

Thursday		

Friday		

Saturday		Special Reminders

Sunday		

Monday	

Tuesday	

Wednesday	

Thursday	

Friday	

Saturday	

Sunday	

Places to Go

- ☐
- ☐
- ☐
- ☐
- ☐
- ☐

People to See

- ☐
- ☐
- ☐
- ☐
- ☐
- ☐

Things to Do

- ☐
- ☐
- ☐
- ☐
- ☐
- ☐
- ☐
- ☐
- ☐
- ☐
- ☐
- ☐

Special Reminders

- ☐
- ☐
- ☐
- ☐
- ☐
- ☐
- ☐

Monday	

Tuesday	

Wednesday	

Thursday	

Friday	

Saturday	

Sunday	

Places to Go

People to See

Things to Do

Special Reminders

Monday

Tuesday

Wednesday

Thursday

Friday

Saturday

Sunday

Places to Go

People to See

Things to Do

Special Reminders

<table>
<tr><td>

Monday

____

____

____

____

Tuesday

____

____

____

Wednesday

____

____

____

____

Thursday

____

____

____

____

____

Friday

____

____

____

____

Saturday

____

____

____

____

Sunday

____

____

____

____

</td><td>

Places to Go

☐ _______________
☐ _______________
☐ _______________
☐ _______________
☐ _______________
☐ _______________

People to See

☐ _______________
☐ _______________
☐ _______________
☐ _______________
☐ _______________
☐ _______________

Things to Do

☐ _______________
☐ _______________
☐ _______________
☐ _______________
☐ _______________
☐ _______________
☐ _______________
☐ _______________
☐ _______________
☐ _______________
☐ _______________
☐ _______________
☐ _______________

Special Reminders

☐ _______________
☐ _______________
☐ _______________
☐ _______________
☐ _______________
☐ _______________

</td></tr>
</table>